What's the Issue?

WHAT'S HACKING?

By Daniel Donato

I0807511

KidHaven PUBLISHING

Published in 2020 by
KidHaven Publishing, an Imprint of Greenhaven Publishing, LLC
353 3rd Avenue
Suite 255
New York, NY 10010

Designer: Deanna Paternostro
Editor: Jennifer Lombardo

Photo credits: Cover (top) Tyler Olson/Shutterstock.com; cover (bottom) REDPIXEL.PL/Shutterstock.com; p. 5 Monkey Business Images/Shutterstock.com; p. 7 Gorodenkoff/Shutterstock.com; p. 9 Donat Sorokin/TASS via Getty Images; p. 11 Paulo Amorim/NurPhoto via Getty Images; p. 13 Greentellect Studio/Shutterstock.com; p. 15 Gladskikh Tatiana/Shutterstock.com; p. 17 rikkyall/Shutterstock.com; p. 19 Jacob Lund/Shutterstock.com; p. 21 s_maria/Shutterstock.com.

Cataloging-in-Publication Data

Names: Donato, Daniel.
Title: What's hacking? / Daniel Donato.
Description: New York : KidHaven Publishing, 2020. | Series: What's the issue? | Includes glossary and index.
Identifiers: ISBN 9781534532335 (pbk.) | ISBN 9781534532212 (library bound) | ISBN 9781534532410 (6 pack) | ISBN 9781534532267 (ebook)
Subjects: LCSH: Hackers–Juvenile literature. | Computer crimes–Juvenile literature. | Computer security–Juvenile literature. | Penetration testing (Computer security)–Juvenile literature. | Computer crimes–Prevention–Juvenile literature.
Classification: LCC HV6773.D668 2020 | DDC 364.16'8–dc23

Printed in the United States of America

CPSIA compliance information: Batch #BW20KL: For further information contact Greenhaven Publishing LLC, New York, New York at 1-844-317-7404.

CONTENTS

Understanding Hacking

Hacking happens when someone gains **access** to a computer system without permission, often through weaknesses known as exploits or vulnerabilities. With this access, a hacker can download people's personal **information**, spy on their activity, or hack into other computers on a **network**.

It's important to know about hacking because computers are a big part of everyday life for people around the world. People's personal information, such as their bank accounts and credit card numbers, is stored on computers. A hacker can target anyone, so knowing how they work is the first step toward **protecting** yourself.

Facing the Facts

Hacking also describes the task of putting together computer parts to make something new that's cool or useful.

Sometimes people hack a computer by looking at a computer's code and finding vulnerabilities. Hackers often work together because the more people and more computers there are working on the job, the faster it can be finished.

Not Like the Movies

In movies and on TV shows, hackers are often shown typing quickly and saying a lot of things about computers that don't seem to make sense. However, in real life, hacking works differently.

Movies and TV shows make hacking look more exciting than it often is in the real world. Real hacking that uses computer code often takes days or even months to finish, and not a lot happens on the computer screen during that time. You wouldn't want to watch that in the middle of a movie or TV show!

Facing the Facts

One of the first movies to show hacking was called *War Games*, which came out in 1983. It's about a young man who hacks into a military computer and accidentally almost starts World War III!

In movies, hacking looks exciting, with a lot of action on screens often watched by a person in a hoodie working in a cool hideout. In reality, most hackers work in their own home, and their work isn't exciting to watch.

Why Do People Hack?

There are a lot of reasons why people try hacking. One reason is to steal information, such as a person's credit card number, to make money. Another is to hurt a person, a company, or even a government the hacker is mad at. Sometimes, they use hacking for **revenge** by making trouble for their target. Other times, they're trying to spread information that will make other people mad and cause changes to happen at a company or in a country.

Hackers can make money by **freezing** a person's or business's computer and making them pay a **ransom** to unfreeze it. Some hackers just do it because they think hacking's fun.

Facing the Facts

When a hacker steals someone's information, they can pretend to be that person. This crime is called identity theft. According to the U.S. government, up to 9 million Americans have their identity stolen every year.

Ransomware locks a person's computer until they pay a ransom. It's a type of malware, which is a combination of the words **malicious** and **software**.

Hacktivism

Hacktivism—a play on the word **activism**—is when someone uses hacking as a form of **political** or social **protest**. One well-known hacktivist group is called Anonymous, which is a word that means "unknown person." Anonymous often targeted people or groups its members thought needed to be brought to justice for doing bad things.

Some people think hacktivism is a good thing because it can create change. Other people think hacktivism is a crime. They don't think anyone except the police should be allowed to decide who gets in trouble for their actions.

Facing the Facts

Hacktivist attacks have decreased, or gone down, by 95 percent since 2015, mostly because Anonymous started to break up.

When members or supporters of Anonymous hold public protests, they wear a special kind of mask (shown here) to hide who they really are.

International Hacking

People or governments from one country sometimes hack into the computer systems of people or governments from another country. Some Russians used hacking in 2016 because they wanted to help Donald Trump get elected U.S. president. Also, hackers from Iran and North Korea have targeted American banks, government **agencies**, and other places.

In the past, wars were fought with guns. Today, many important things are controlled by computers, so it makes sense for one government to use hacking to take control of another country's computers from far away. This is a new kind of war.

Facing the Facts

In 2014, Sony Pictures Entertainment was hacked, and new movies were put online before anyone was meant to see them. Later, it was found that a North Korean group did this because one of Sony's movies poked fun at North Korea's leader, Kim Jong-Un.

The United States has also targeted other countries. In 2019, it hacked Russia's electric power supply. These wires, which send electricity to homes and businesses, are controlled by computers today.

Social Engineering

Hacking a computer's code is hard work, so most hacking is done through social engineering, which is easier. This happens when a hacker tricks someone into giving them information they can use to get into the person's accounts or computer. Social engineering works because most people don't think that someone might be trying to trick them.

One way people use social engineering is on **social media**. Have you ever taken an online quiz that asked you to log in to Facebook to get your results? If the quiz is made by a hacker, the page at the end asking for your login information is fake. Your email and password would go right to the hacker if you entered them.

Facing the Facts

Social engineering is sometimes called scamming. Real businesses warn customers that only scammers will ask someone to give their credit card number over the phone.

Older people are often targeted by hackers because they don't always know a lot about how computers work. One common trick is to call someone and tell them their computer has a problem and they need to follow directions to fix it. Those directions make the person download malware the hacker can use.

Phishing

Phishing is a kind of social engineering that uses email to get someone's information. A hacker may send an email that looks like it's from a real company, asking you to click a link, or you may get an email from someone you don't know, asking you to lend them money.

If someone online asks for any of your personal information, think about why they're asking! If the questions come from a friend, call or text them about it. If they were hacked already, the hackers might be using their email or social media accounts to hack other people they know by pretending to be them.

Facing the Facts

People who work with computers say that phishing emails make up about 91 percent of all attacks on computers and are how 92 percent of all malware gets on people's computers.

These are just some ways hackers can get your personal information.

Hacking as a Job

Some people get jobs as hackers. These people, who are also known as "white hat," or **ethical**, hackers, are hired to test the security of a company's computers. They tell the company about any vulnerabilities they find and how they can be fixed.

To be a white hat hacker, someone needs to be good at solving, or coming up with answers to, problems. They also need to take classes in computer science and be good at thinking like a "black hat" hacker, or someone who uses hacking illegally. Some white hat hackers are very good at it because they used to be black hat hackers!

Facing the Facts

A hackathon sounds like an event for hackers, but it's actually a way for people to experiment with new software or computer code and learn the basics of something new within one or two days.

White hat hackers help make companies' computer security better so their customers' information is safe from black hat hackers.

Using Common Sense

It can be scary to know that someone might want to hack into your computer. However, remember that most hackers count on people giving them what they want. Hackers who try to use vulnerabilities in computer code generally go after big companies, not regular people.

By using common sense, people can make their chances of getting hacked much smaller. If something sounds too good to be true, it probably is! If you think something might be a scam, look it up. Other people talk about scams online. If you Google something and the word "scam" pops up after it, be very careful.

Facing the Facts

According to CNN, personal information everyone should keep private on the internet includes their name, email address, phone number, birthday, passwords, and home address.

WHAT CAN YOU DO?

Talk to your parents and grandparents about hacking.

Keep private information to yourself, even if it doesn't seem important.

Don't click on links or attachments in emails, even from a friend, unless you were expecting to get them.

Learn about how computers work, and read about common scams so you can tell when someone is trying to trick you.

Never respond to someone who asks you for money, even if they promise you more money in return.

Don't download things from unofficial websites.

Learning about hacking is the first step toward protecting yourself from it.

GLOSSARY

access: The ability to use or have something.

activism: Taking action to support or oppose something.

agency: A government department that is responsible for a certain activity or area.

ethical: Following accepted rules of behavior; morally right and good.

freeze: To stop something from working as it should.

information: Knowledge or facts about something.

malicious: Purposely trying to do harm.

network: A group of computers that can send information to each other.

political: Relating to government and beliefs about how governments should work.

protect: To keep safe.

protest: A way of showing disapproval of something.

ransom: Money that is paid to free something that has been captured.

revenge: Doing harm in return for a wrong.

social media: A collection of websites and applications, or apps, that allow users to interact with each other and create online communities.

software: Programs that run on computers and perform certain functions.

FOR MORE INFORMATION

WEBSITES

Girls Who Code

girlswhocode.com

Learning about coding is one way to learn how to keep your computer safe from hackers—and anyone can do it!

Kids Hack Day

www.kidshackday.com

Find a hackathon near you using this website.

BOOKS

Hudak, Heather C. *Helpful Hackers*. Minneapolis, MN: Abdo Publishing, 2019.

Smith, Jonathan. *White Hat Hacking*. New York, NY: Cavendish Square, 2015.

Vorderman, Carol. *Computer Coding: Python Games for Kids*. London, England: Dorling Kindersley Limited, 2018.

Publisher's note to educators and parents: Our editors have carefully reviewed these websites to ensure that they are suitable for students. Many websites change frequently, however, and we cannot guarantee that a site's future contents will continue to meet our high standards of quality and educational value. Be advised that students should be closely supervised whenever they access the Internet.

INDEX